COLLECTED ANIMAL POEMS VOLUME I
The Iron Wolf

COLLECTED ANIMAL POEMS

Ted Hughes

COLLECTED ANIMAL POEMS

VOLUME 1

The Iron Wolf

Illustrated by Chris Riddell

faber and faber

LONDON · BOSTON

First published in Great Britain in 1995
by Faber and Faber Limited
3 Queen Square London WC1N 3AU

Phototypeset by Wilmaset Ltd, Birkenhead, Wirral
Printed in England by Clays Ltd, St Ives plc

A CIP record for this book
is available from the British Library

ISBN 0–571–16451–x (cased)
    0–571–17622–4 (pbk)

10 9 8 7 6 5 4 3 2

to Olwyn and Gerald

Contents

Amulet

Inside the Wolf's fang, the mountain of heather.
Inside the mountain of heather, the Wolf's fur.
Inside the Wolf's fur, the ragged forest.
Inside the ragged forest, the Wolf's foot.
Inside the Wolf's foot, the stony horizon.
Inside the stony horizon, the Wolf's tongue.
Inside the Wolf's tongue, the Doe's tears.
Inside the Doe's tears, the frozen swamp.
Inside the frozen swamp, the Wolf's blood.
Inside the Wolf's blood, the snow wind.
Inside the snow wind, the Wolf's eye.
Inside the Wolf's eye, the North Star.
Inside the North Star, the Wolf's fang.

The Mermaid's Purse

The Mermaid's shriek
Made Ocean shake.

She'd opened her purse
For an aspirin –
What a shock!
Out came a shark
With a great black fin
Hissing: 'Here's Nurse
And Surgeon in one
Great flashing grin!'

Now both headache
And head have gone
Or she'd feel worse.

Limpet

When big surf slams
His tower so hard
The lighthouse-keeper's
Teeth are jarred,

The Limpet laughs
Beneath her hat:
'There's nothing I love
So much as that!

Huge seas of shock
That roar to knock me
Off my rocker
Rock me, rock me.'

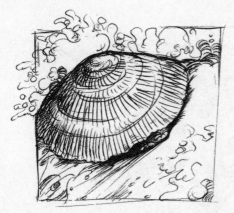

Whale

O hear the Whale's
Colossal song!
Suppler than any
Soprano's tongue

And wild as a hand
Among harp strings
Plunging through all
The seas she sings.

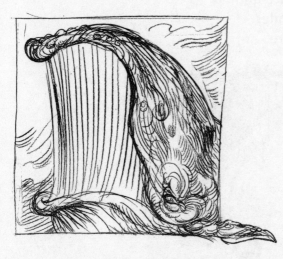

Conger Eel

I am Conger
Out in the rough.
Long enough
But growing longer –
Thicker too.
A bit of a shock
At my cave door
Beneath my rock.

But look at you –
You're not so thin.
As for my grin –
Your teeth are quite a
Good bit whiter.
And eat more.

Lobster

This is the Lobster's song:
'Has anybody seen a
Heavy-duty knight
Dancing through the fight
Like a ballerina?
I was a thrilling sight!
Alas, not for long!

It was the stupid sea,
The fumbling, mumbling sea,
The sea took me apart
And lost my clever wits
And lost my happy heart
And then jammed all the bits
Back together wrong.
Now I'm just a fright.
I don't know what to do.
I'm feeling pretty blue.'

Sandflea

'O see my eyes!'
The Sandflea cries,
'So beautiful,
So blue, they make
The sea seem dull.'

But then she hides
Beneath the wrack.
She hears the tide's
Wild cry – 'Give back
That China blue
I lent to you' –
As it sweeps blind hands
Of scrabbling suds
Across the sands.

Cormorant

Drowned fishermen come back
  As famished cormorants
With bare and freezing webby toes
  Instead of boots and pants.

You've a hook at the end of your nose.
  You shiver all the day
Trying to dry your oilskin pyjamas
  Under the icy spray.

But worst – O worst of all –
  The moment that you wish
For fried fish fingers in a flash
  You're gagged with a frozen fish.

Whelk

I wonder whether
Whelks can wish?
If I were a whelk
I think I'd sulk
To be a fish.

Though anything other
Than a screw
Of rubbery chew,
A gurgle of goo
Going down a drain,
Would be a gain.

Heron

I am nothing
But a prayer
To catch a fish.
A hush of air –

A bloom of cloud
On a tilting stalk.
Over the water's face
I walk.

The little fishes
Tucked in under
Missing my flash
Sleep through my thunder.

Starfish

A Starfish stares
At stars that pour
Through depths of space
Without a shore.

She crimps her fingertips
And cries:
'If I could weep enough
Maybe
To rinse the salt
Out of my eyes
One of those dazzlers
Would be me.'

Sea Anemone

For such a dainty face
A touch is like a danger.
But the dance of my many arms
To the music of the sea
Brings many a friend to me.

None can resist my grace.
All fall for my charms.

Many a friend, many a stranger,
Many an enemy
Melts in my embrace.
I am anemone.

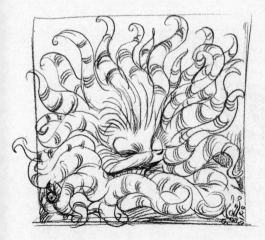

Crab

In low tide pools
I pack myself like
A handy pocket
Chest of tools.

But as the tide fills
Dancing I go
Under lifted veils
Tiptoe, tiptoe.

And with pliers and pincers
Repair and remake
The daintier dancers
The breakers break.

Jellyfish

When my chandelier
Waltzes pulsing near
Let the swimmer fear.

Beached and bare
I'm less of a scare.
But I don't care.

Though I look like a slob
It's a delicate job
Being just a blob.

Ragworm

Ragworm once
Was all the rage.
But suddenly, see
This foolish age
Of fish is in.
Fashion of flounce,
Of scale and slime,
Of scoot and squirm
And gill and fin
Gawping like fools.

Let future time
Be soon unfurled.

Bring all such schools
To end of term.

Return the world
To me, the Worm.

Octopus

'I am your bride,'
The Octopus cried.
'O jump from your vessel!
O dive with your muscle
Through Ocean's rough bustle!
Though I look like a tassel
Of hideous gristle,
A tussle of hassle,
I'm a bundle of charms.
O come, let us wrestle
With noses a-jostle!
You'll swoon in my arms
With a sigh like a whistle – '

And she waved her arms, waiting,
Her colours pulsating
Like strobe lights rotating,

Her huge eyes dilating . . .

Blenny

Ocean's great hammer
Shatters itself
All to forge
This wiry wee elf.

Flounder

The Flounder sees
Through crooked eyes.
Through crooked lips
The Flounder cries:

'While other fish flee
In goggling fright
From horrors below
And to left and to right

I lie here
With a lovely feeling
Flat on my back
And gaze at the ceiling.'

Shrimp

The Shrimp sings: 'The sea's
Ugliest weather
Merely preens
My glassy feather.

I have the surf
As a rocking chair,
Combers to comb
My dainty hair,

Though it's true my meat
Is a bit too sweet
And all who happen to meet me
Eat me.'

Gull

What yanks upward your line of sight –
Is it a clifftop, soaring kite?

Only a Blackback Gull
Giving your eye a pull.

Hermit Crab

The sea-bed's great –
But it's a plate.
Every fish
Watches this dish.

Just to be tough
Is not enough.
Some of the smart
Don't even start.

'I stay in bed
With my house on my head,'
Says the Hermit Crab,
'Or go by cab.'

Mussel

When you prise
Her shells apart
To say Hello
The Mussel cries:
'I know! I know!
I confess
I am a mess.
But I'm all heart –
Heart that could not
Softer soften!

An ugly girl,
But often, often
With a pearl.'

Seal

Where Ocean heaved
A breast of silk
And a black jag reef
Boiled into milk

There bobbed up a head
With eyes as wild
And wide and dark
As a famine child.

I thought, by the way
It stared at me,
It had lost its mother
In the sea.

The Osprey

The fierce Osprey
Prays over the bay.

God hides below
In his shadow.

Let God reveal
His scaly, cold
And shining brow –
.

Osprey shall fold
His wings and bow
His head and kneel.

Fantails

Up on the roof the Fantail Pigeons dream
Of dollops of curled cream.

At every morning window their soft voices
Comfort all the bedrooms with caresses.

'Peace, peace, peace,' through the day
The Fantails hum and murmur and pray.

Like a dream, where resting angels crowded
The roof-slope, that has not quite faded.

When they clatter up, and veer, and soar in a ring
It's as if the house suddenly sang something.

The cats of the house, purring on lap and knee,
Dig their claws and scowl with jealousy.

Worm

Lowly, slowly,
A pink, wet worm
Sings in the rain:
'O see me squirm

Along the path.
I warp and wind.
I'm searching hard.
If I could find

My elbow, my hair,
My hat, my shoe,
I'd look as pretty
As you, and you.'

Thrush

The speckled Thrush
With a cheerful shout
Dips his beak in the dark
And lifts the sun out.

Then he calls to the Snails:
'God's here again!
Close your eyes for prayers
While I sing Amen.

And after Amen
Rejoice! Rejoice!'

Then he scoops up some dew
And washes his voice.

Otter

An Otter am I,
High and dry
Over the pebbles
See me hobble.
My water-bag wobbles
Until I spill
At the river sill
And flow away thin
As an empty skin
That dribbles bubbles.

Then I jut up my mutt,
All spiky with wet.
My moustaches bristle
As I mutter, or whistle:
'Now what's the matter?'

(For that is my song.
Not very long.
There might be a better
Some wetter, wittier
Otter could utter.)

Owl

Owl! Owl!
A merry lad!
When he thinks 'Good!'
It comes out 'Bad!'

The poor Mouse cries:
'Please let me go!'
And Owl thinks 'Yes'
But it comes out 'No!

OH NO! OH NO!
OH NO! OH NO!
HO HO! HO HO!
HO HO! HO HO!

O rest your head,
You silly fellow,
Upon this lovely
Feather pillow!'

Dragonfly

Now let's have another try
To love the giant Dragonfly.

Stand beside the peaceful water.
Next thing – a whispy, dry clatter

And he whizzes to a dead stop
In mid-air, and his eyes pop.

Snaky stripes, a snaky fright!
Does he sting? Does he bite?

Suddenly he's gone. Suddenly back. A
Scary jumping cracker –

Here! Right here!
An inch from your ear!

Sizzling in the air
And giving you a stare

Out of the huge cockpit of his eyes – !

Now say: 'What a lovely surprise!'

Snail

With skin all wrinkled
Like a Whale
On a ribbon of sea
Comes the moonlit Snail.

The Cabbage murmurs:
'I feel something's wrong!'
The Snail says: 'Shhh!
I am God's tongue.'

The Rose shrieks out:
'What's this? O what's this?'
The Snail says: 'Shhh!
I am God's kiss.'

So the whole garden
(Till stars fail)
Suffers the passion
Of the Snail.

The Red Admiral

This butterfly
Was the ribbon tie

On the Paradise box
Of Paradise chocs.

O where's the girl
Who wouldn't go bare

As a thistle to wear
Such a bow in her hair?

Ram

When a Ram can't sleep
He doesn't count sheep.

He blinks, blinks, blinks,
And he thinks, thinks, thinks

'How has it come to be
That I'm the only me?

I am, I am, I am
Since I was first a lamb.

But where was I before?'

Then he snores a gentle snore

And hears, deep in his sleep,
A million million sheep

Each one bleating: 'Why
Am I the only I?'

Stickleback

The Stickleback's a spiky chap,
  Worse than a bit of briar.
Hungry Pike would sooner swallow
  Embers from a fire.

The Stickleback is fearless in
  The way he loves his wife.
Every minute of the day
  He guards her with his life.

She, like him, is dressed to kill
  In stiff and steely prickles,
And when they kiss, there bubbles up
  The laughter of the tickles.

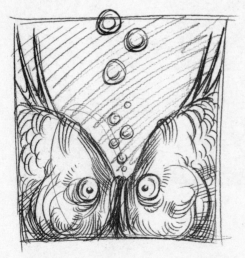

Toad

The Toad cries: 'First I was a thought.
Then that thought it grew a wart.
And the wart had thoughts
Which turned to warts.

I tried to flee
This warty wart
With froggy jumps
But the wart got mumps.
Now this is me.
This lump of bumps
I have to be.

My consolation prize
Is ten-candlepower eyes.
But where are all the flies?
Eaten by those damned bats!'

His eyes pull down their hats.

Robin

When wind brings more snow
To deepen deep snow

Robin busies his beak.
But the pickings are bleak.

He stands at your open door
Asking for more.

'Anything edible?'
He stares towards the table.

The cat can't believe
A bird could be so naive.

Half-shut eye, wide ear
She prays: 'Let him come near!'

Then, with his flaming shirt
Telling him nothing can hurt,

And that he will always win,
Robin bounces in.

Cow

The Cow comes home swinging
Her udder and singing:

'The dirt O the dirt
It does me no hurt.

And a good splash of muck
Is a blessing of luck.

O I splosh through the mud
But the breath of my cud

Is sweeter than silk.
O I splush through manure

But my heart stays pure
As a pitcher of milk.'

Peacock

A perfect Peacock on the lawn
  Pranced proudly through his paces.
Pecked at old pancakes, flared his fan
  Like a hand of neon aces.

But while we smiled, he sidled in
  To the nursery flowerbed.
With quivering crown and scabby cheeks
  He pecked off every head.

He slept in the wood. His shawl of eyes
  Drooped to the woodland floor.
O much as we admired his plumes
  A Fox admired him more.

Pig

I am the Pig.

I saw in my sleep
A dreadful egg.

What a thing to have seen!
And what can it mean

That the Sun's red eye
Which seems to fry
In the dawn sky
So frightens me?

Why should that be?
The meaning is deep.

Upward at these
Hard mysteries

A humble hog
I gape agog.

Sparrow

Sparrow squats in the dust
Begging for a crust.

'Help an old soldier,' he cries.
He doesn't care if he lies.

All he wears on his back
Is a raggy sack.

All day the same old shout:
'I'm back from the wars, worn out!'

Though it looks like shirking
He works at it like working.

Later, on the chimney pot
He takes his sauna very hot.

Mole

I am the Mole.
Not easy to know.
Wherever I go
I travel by hole.

My hill-making hand
Is the best of me.
As a seal under sea
I swim under land.

My nose hunts bright
As a beam of light.
With the prick of a pin
My eyes were put in.

Your telly's there.
You feast as you stare.
Worms are my diet.
In dark and in quiet

I don't eat alone.
At my table sit
Centurion
And Ancient Brit.

Donkey

The Horse on giant, steely springs
Bounds all over the place.
It circles and circles and circles the globe
In an endless, panting race.

But the Donkey's huge strength
Is already here
At the end of the Horse's journeys,
Asleep, drooping one ear.

Goat

Bones. Belly. Bag.
All ridge, all sag.
Lumps of torn hair
Glued here and there.

What else am I
With my wicked eye?

Though nobly born
With a lofty nose
I'm as happy with the Thorn
As I am with the Rose.

Pike

I am the Pike.
O you who walk
On two legs and talk
Do not know what I'm like.

You think I'm a cruel
Robot shark
Grabbing fish in the dark
To be my fuel.

No, no! I laze
Through the blazing June days.

On, on, all summer
I sunbathe in bliss
And gaze at the sky
And pray to become a
Dragonfly.

Remember this
When you say that my fangs
Are solid hunger pangs,
And that my work
Is murder in the murk,
And that I draw my wages
In the Dark Ages.

Squirrel

With a rocketing rip
Squirrel will zip
Up a tree-bole
As if down a hole.

He jars to a stop
With tingling ears.
He has two gears:
Freeze and top.

Then up again, plucky
As a jockey
Galloping a race-
Horse into space.

Crow

Thrice, thrice, thrice, the coal-bright Crow
Baaarks–aaarks–aaarks, like a match being struck
To look for trouble.

    'Hear ye the Preacher:
    Nature to Nature
    Returns each creature.'

The Crow lifts a claw –
A crucifix
Of burnt matchsticks.

    'I am the Priest.
    For my daily bread
    I nurse the dead.'

The monkish Crow
Ruffles his cloak
Like a burnt bible.

    'At my humble feast
    I am happy to drink
    Whatever you think.'

Then the Crow
Laughs through his hacker
And grows blacker.

Hen

Dowdy the Hen
Has nothing to do
But peer and peck, and peck and peer
At nothing.

Sometimes a couple of scratches to right
Sometimes a couple of scratches to left
And sometimes a head-up, red-rimmed stare
At nothing.

O Hen in your pen, O Hen, O when
Will something happen?
Nothing to do but brood on her nest
And wish.

Wish? Wish? What shall she wish for?
Stealthy fingers
Under her bum.
An egg on your dish.

Shrew

Shrill and astonishing the shrew
Dashes through the early dew.

He's a famine on four feet:
Something to eat! Something to eat!

His scream is thinner than a pin
And hurts your ear when it goes in.

And when he meets another shrew
He doesn't rear on hinder toes

And nose to tender, waggling nose
Gently ask: 'How do you do?'

He draws a single, furious breath
And fights the other to the death.

Cat

You need your Cat.
When you slump down
All tired and flat
With too much town

With too many lifts
Too many floors
Too many neon-lit
Corridors

Too many people
Telling you what
You just must do
And what you must not

With too much headache
Video glow
Too many answers
You never will know

Then stroke the Cat
That warms your knee
You'll find her purr
Is a battery

For into your hands
Will flow the powers
Of the beasts who ignore
These ways of ours

And you'll be refreshed
Through the Cat on your lap
With a Leopard's yawn
And a Tiger's nap.

Cuckoo

The Cuckoo's the crookedest, wickedest bird.
His song has two notes, but only one word.

He says to the Linnet: 'Your eggs look so ill!
Now I am the doctor, and here is my pill.'

Within that pill, the Cuckoo-child
Crouches hidden, wicked and wild.

He bursts his shell, and with weightlifter's legs
He flings from the nest the Linnet's eggs.

Then bawls to the Linnet: 'Look at me, Mam!
How quickly I've grown, and how hungry I am!'

She thinks he is hers, she is silly with joy.
She wears herself bare for the horrible boy.

Till one day he burps, with a pitiless laugh,
'I've had enough of this awful caf!'

And away he whirls, to Cuckoo-land,
And leaves her to weep with
   a worm in her hand.

The Heron

The Sun's an iceberg
In the sky.
In solid freeze
The fishes lie.

Doomed is the Dab.
Death leans above –

But the Heron
Poised to stab
Has turned to iron
And cannot move.

The Wolverine

The gleeful, evil Wolverine
   Lopes along.
'O I am going to devour everybody and everything!'
   Is his song.

With gloating cackle the glutton gobbles
   The eagle's brood.
Snaps the snoring snowy owl's head off, chuckling
   'This is good!'

The trapped wolf's pelt shall not adorn
   The trapper's wall.
The Wolverine's gulped it down with a wild laugh,
   Nails and all.

When he bobs up in the Northern Lights
   With more merry tales
The bear feels the skull creak under his scalp
   And his smile fails.

The gleeful, evil Wolverine
   Belly full of song
Sings: 'I am coming to swallow you all, Hiya!'
   Loping along.

Brooktrout

The Brooktrout, superb as a matador,
Sways invisibly there
In water empty as air.

The Brooktrout leaps, splendid as a leopard,
But dropping back into swift glass
Resumes clear nothingness.

The numb-cold current's brainwave is lightning –
No good gasping 'Look!'
It vanished as it struck.

You can catch Brooktrout, a goggling gewgaw,
But never the flash God made
Drawing the river's blade.

The Snow-shoe Hare

The Snow-shoe Hare
Is his own sudden blizzard.

Or he comes, limping after the snow storm,
A big, lost, left-behind snowflake
Crippled with bandages.

White, he is looking for a great whiteness
To hide in.
But the starry night is on his track.

His own dogged shadow
Panics him to right, then to left, then backwards,
Then forwards –
Till he skids skittering
Out across the blue ice, meeting the Moon.

He stretches up, craning slender
Listening
For the Fox's icicles and the White Owl's frore cloud.

In his popping eyes
The whole crowded heaven struggles softly.

Glassy mountains, breathless, brittle forests
Are frosty aerials
Balanced in his ears.

And his nose bobs wilder
And his heart thuds harder

Tethered there, so hotly
To his crouching shadow.

Ants

Can an Ant love an Ant?
Can a scissor-face
Kiss a scissor-face?
Can an Ant smile? It can't.

Why all that coming and going?
They run, they wave their arms, they cry –
The Ants' nest is a nunnery
Of holy madwomen.

They race out, searching for God.
They race home: 'He's not there!'
And their mad heads nod, nod, nod,
And they stagger in despair.

Bicycling, weeping, trembling (once
To have lost your last hope yet to
Still have just a chance
Is enough to know what they go through)

And carrying such a sob
Inside a body that's
Part hard little knots
And part a scalding blob

Of molten copper trickling
Through a burning house.

Love of God is fierce!

But the Sun's great yokel, Earth, only yawns and
  scratches the tickling.

The Arctic Fox

No feet. Snow.
Ear – a star-cut
Ache of air.
The world hangs watched.

Jaws flimsy as ice
Champ at the hoar-frost
Of something tasteless –
A snowflake of feathers.

The forest sighs.
A fur of breath
Empty as moonlight
Has a blue shadow.

A dream twitches
The sleeping face
Of the snowlit land.

When day wakes
Sun will not find
What night hardly noticed.

Woodpecker

Woodpecker is rubber-necked
   But has a nose of steel.
He bangs his head against the wall
   And cannot even feel.

When Woodpecker's jack-hammer head
   Starts up its dreadful din
Knocking the dead bough double dead
   How do his eyes stay in?

Pity the poor dead oak that cries
   In terrors and in pains.
But pity more Woodpecker's eyes
   And bouncing rubber brains.

The Moorhen

Might not notice you.
She's policing the water-bugs
In her municipal uniform.

A watchful clockwork
Jerks her head ahead, to inspect ahead
At each deep tread
Of her giant ooze-treading clawspread.

Her undertail flirts, jerk by jerk,
A chevron blaze, her functionary flash,
And the blood-orange badge or bleb
On her helmet neb
Lets the transgressing water-skeeter know
The arresting face, the stabbing body-blow
Is official.

Her legs are still primeval –
Toy-grotesque
As when she – black, thistledown, tip-toe
Scampered across the picture-skin of water.

Lumpier now, she sprint-strides into flight
Across stepping stones of slapped circles

Then dangles her drape of webs below her
Like a hawthorn fly, till she hoicks up
Clear over the bull-rush plumes, and crash-drops

Into her off-duty nervous collapse.

Wolf

The Iron Wolf, the Iron Wolf

Stands on the world with jagged fur.
The rusty Moon rolls through the sky.
The iron river cannot stir.
The iron wind leaks out a cry

Caught in the barbed and iron wood.
The Iron Wolf runs over the snow
Looking for a speck of blood.
Only the Iron Wolf shall know

The iron of his fate.
He lifts his nose and moans,
Licks the world clean as a plate
And leaves his own bones.

Eagle

Big wings dawn dark.
The Sun is hunting.
Thunder collects, under granite eyebrows.

The horizons are ravenous.
The dark mountain has an electric eye.
The Sun lowers its meat-hook.

His spread fingers measure a heaven, then a
    heaven.
His ancestors worship only him,
And his children's children cry to him alone.

His trapeze is a continent.
The Sun is looking for fuel
With the gaze of a guillotine.

And already the White Hare crouches at the sacrifice,
Already the Fawn stumbles to offer itself up
And the Wolf-cub weeps to be chosen.

The huddle-shawled lightning-faced warrior
Stamps his shaggy-trousered dance
On an altar of blood.

Mooses

The goofy Moose, the walking house-frame,
Is lost
In the forest. He bumps, he blunders, he stands.

With massy bony thoughts sticking out near his
    ears –
Reaching out palm upwards, to catch whatever
    might be falling from heaven –
He tries to think,
Leaning their huge weight
On the lectern of his front legs.

He can't find the world!
Where did it go? What does a world look like?
The Moose
Crashes on, and crashes into a lake, and stares at
    the mountain and cries:
'Where do I belong? This is no place!'

He turns dragging half the lake out after him
And charges the cackling underbrush –

He meets another Moose
He stares, he thinks: 'It's only a mirror!'

'Where is the world?' he groans. 'O my lost world!
And why am I so ugly?
And why am I so far away from my feet?'

He weeps.
Hopeless drops drip from his droopy lips.

The other Moose just stands there doing the same.

Two dopes of the deep woods.

Puma

God put the Cougar on the mountain
To be the organist
Of the cathedral-shaped echoes.

Her screams play the hollow cliffs, the brinks
And the abyss.
Her music amazes the acoustics.

She lifts the icy shivering summit
Of her screech
And climbs it, looking for her Maker.

A crazy-gaze priestess of caverns –
All night she tries to break into heaven
With a song like a missile, while the Moon frosts
    her face.

All day afterwards, worn out,
She sleeps in the sun.

Sometimes – half-melted
In the sheet-flame silence –
Opens one jewel.

Phoenix

The funny Phoenix
Is no Sphinx
Rotting forever
In Egypt's stinks.

When his sun sets
He does not sulk
And sink in sands
His deathless bulk

But blazing in perfume
Like the morn
He eats himself roasted
And is reborn.

The Musk Ox

Express blizzards rumble, a horizontal snow-
    haulage,
Over the roof of the world.
The weathercock up there
Is the Musk Ox, in his ankle-length hair.

Under the skyslide avalanche of white darkness,
    under walloping wheels of wind
He clings to his eyes –
A little castle with two windows
Like a fish on the bed of a flood-river.

The stars are poor company.
They huddle deep in their aeons, only just
    managing to exist,
Jostled by every gust,
Pinned precariously to their flutters of light,
Tense and weightless, ready to be snatched away
    into some other infinity.

And the broken tree-dwarves, in their hollow,
    near him,
Have no cheer to spare,
Just hanging on, not daring to think of the
    bottomless emptiness of the blast
That shakes them by the nape and pounds their
    shoulders.

And the mountains stare
Towards him fadingly
Like solid-frozen Mammoths staring at a Coca-
Cola sign.
And the seas, heaping and freezing, neighbour
him unknowingly
Like whales
Shouldering round a lost champagne cork.

He's happy.
Bowed beneath his snowed-under lean-to of
horns,
Hunched over his nostrils, singing to himself,
Happy inside there, bent at his hearth-glow
Over the simple picture book
Of himself
As he was yesterday, as he will be tomorrow

While the Pole groans
And skies slither off the world's edge and the
stars cling to each other.

Goose

The White Bear, with smoking mouth, embraces
All the North.
The Wild Goose listens.

South, south –
                 the Goose stretches his neck
Over the glacier,

And high, high
Turns the globe in his hands.

Hunts with his pack from star to star.
Sees the sun far down behind the world.

Sinks through fingers of light, with apricot breast,
To startle sleeping farms, at apple dawn,
With iceberg breath.

Then to and fro all Christmas, evening and
   morning,
Urging his linked team,
Clears the fowler's gun and the surf angler.

Homesick
Smells the first flower of the Northern Lights –

Clears the Lamb's cry, wrestles heaven,
Sets the globe turning.

Clears the dawns – a compass tolling
North, north.
                    North, north.

Wingbeat wading the flame of evening.

Till he dips his eyes
In the whale's music

Among the boom
Of calving glaciers

And wooing of wolves
And rumpus of walrus.

The Honey Bee

The Honey Bee
Brilliant as Einstein's idea
Can't be taught a thing.
Like the Sun, she's on course forever.

As if nothing else at all existed
Except her flowers.
No mountains, no cows, no beaches, no shops.
Only the rainbow waves of her flowers

A tremor in emptiness

A flying carpet of flowers

                           – a pattern
Coming and going – very loosely woven –
Out of which she works her solutions.

Furry goblin midgets
(The beekeeper's thoughts) clamber stickily
Over the Sun's face – gloves of shadow.

But the Honey Bee
Cannot imagine him, in her brilliance,

Though he's a stowaway on her carpet of colour-
 waves
And drinks her sums.

Grizzly

I see a Bear
Growing out of a bulb in wet soil licks its black tip
With a pink tongue its little eyes
Open and see a present an enormous bulging
    mystery package
Over which it walks sniffing at seams
Digging at the wrapping overjoyed holding the
    joy off sniffing and scratching
Teasing itself with scrapings and lickings and the
    thought of it
And little sips of the ecstasy of it

O Bear do not open your package
Sit on your backside and sunburn your belly
It is all there it has actually arrived
No matter how long you dawdle it cannot get
    away
Shamble about lazily laze there in the admiration
    of it
With all the insects it's attracted all going crazy
And those others the Squirrel with its pop-eyed
    amazement
The Deer with its pop-eyed incredulity
The Weasel pop-eyed with envy and trickery
All going mad for a share wave them off laze

Yawn and grin let your heart thump happily
Warm your shining cheek fur in the morning sun

You have got it everything for nothing

In the Likeness of a Grasshopper

A trap
Waits on the field path.

A wicker contraption, with working parts,
Its spring tensed and set.

So flimsily made, out of grass
(Out of the stems, the joints, the raspy dry flags).

Baited with a fur-soft caterpillar,
A belly of amorous life, pulsing signals.

Along comes a love-sick, perfume-footed
Music of the wild earth.

The trap, touched by a breath,
Jars into action, its parts blur –

And music cries out.

A sinewy violin
Has caught its violinist.

Cloud-fingered summer, the beautiful trapper,
Picks up the singing cage

And takes out the Song, adds it to the Songs
With which she robes herself, which are her wealth,

Sets her trap again, a yard further on.

Spider

On the whole, people dislike spiders.
Where is my book of spiders? A book of devotions
Penned by a passionate heart,
By a dedicated priest of the spider.

The anatomy – so prodigal in wonders!
And the strategies for reproduction,
For gratifying the hungers, beggar belief.
Web-weaving
Is the slightest of the spider's talents
Compared to the feats of prestidigitation
That usher his offspring to their independence.
The web is part acronym, part phone,
Part boutique front for the real business –
A sparkle of his virtuoso wit
Cast over trifles, to beguile fools.

Even so, he's ignorant of his best art,
Which is to dangle, on his invisible harness,
On to my page, from my hair.
Then the thought 'Thank God – I'm in for some
    luck!'
Really startles me.
And for a whole hour after, I feel much better
And, though he doesn't feel it, I love him.

Crow's Elephant Totem Song

Once upon a time
God made this Elephant.
Then it was delicate and small
It was not freakish at all
Or melancholy

The Hyenas sang in the scrub: 'You are beautiful' –
They showed their scorched heads and grinning
    expressions
Like the half-rotted stumps of amputations –
'We envy your grace
Waltzing through the thorny growth
O take us with you to the Land of Peaceful
O ageless eyes of innocence and kindliness
Lift us from the furnaces
And furies of our blackened faces
Within these hells we writhe
Shut in behind the bars of our teeth
In hourly battle with a death
The size of the earth
Having the strength of the earth.'

So the Hyenas ran under the Elephant's tail
As like a lithe and rubber oval
He strolled gladly around inside his ease
But he was not God no it was not his
To correct the damned
In rage in madness then they lit their mouths

They tore out his entrails
They divided him among their several hells
To cry all his separate pieces
Swallowed and inflamed
Amidst paradings of infernal laughter.

At the Resurrection
The Elephant got himself together with correction
Deadfall feet and toothproof body and bulldozing
    bones
And completely altered brains
Behind aged eyes, that were wicked and wise.

So through the orange blaze and blue shadow
Of the afterlife, effortless and immense,
The Elephant goes his own way, a walking sixth
    sense,
And opposite and parallel
The sleepless Hyenas go
Along a leafless skyline trembling like an oven roof
With a whipped run
Their shame-flags tucked hard down
Over the gutsacks
Crammed with putrefying laughter
Blotched black with the leakage and seepings
And they sing: 'Ours is the land
Of loveliness and beautiful
Is the putrid mouth of the leopard

And the graves of fever
Because it is all we have – '
And they vomit their laughter.

And the Elephant sings deep in the forest-maze
About a star of deathless and painless peace
But no astronomer can find where it is.

Sources

The poems in this book were first published in the following
   collections:

Moon-bells (Chatto & Windus, 1978): Grizzly (under the title 'I See a
   Bear').
Under the North Star (Faber and Faber, 1981): Amulet; The Osprey;
   The Heron; The Wolverine; Brooktrout; The Snow-shoe Hare;
   The Arctic Fox; Woodpecker; Wolf; Eagle; Mooses; Puma; The
   Musk Ox; Goose.
River (Faber and Faber, 1983): The Moorhen.
Flowers and Insects (Faber and Faber, 1986): The Honey Bee; In the
   Likeness of a Grasshopper.
The Cat and the Cuckoo (Sunstone Press, 1987): Fantails; Worm;
   Thrush; Otter; Owl; Dragonfly; Snail; Ram; The Red Admiral;
   Stickleback; Toad; Robin; Cow; Peacock; Pig; Sparrow; Mole;
   Donkey; Pike; Goat; Squirrel; Crow; Hen; Shrew; Cat; Cuckoo.
Crow (Faber and Faber, 1972): Crow's Elephant Totem Song.
Uncollected: The Mermaid's Purse; Limpet; Whale; Conger Eel;
   Lobster; Sandflea; Cormorant; Whelk; Heron; Starfish; Sea
   Anemone; Crab; Jellyfish; Ragworm; Octopus; Blenny; Flounder;
   Shrimp; Gull; Hermit Crab; Mussel; Seal; Ants; Spider.

Index of First Lines

[88]

When you prise 21
Where Ocean heaved 22
With a rocketing rip 46
With skin all wrinkled 30
Woodpecker is rubber-necked 61

You need your Cat 50

Subject Index

This index refers readers to all four volumes of the *Collected Animal Poems*. Numbers in **bold** refer to volume numbers. Individual birds, fish and insects are listed under the category headings BIRDS, FISH and INSECTS.

black rhino 4:50
bull *see under* cow
bullfrog 3:111

calf *see under* cow
cat 1:50; 2:98
  kitten 3:7
cougar 1:68
cow 1:37; 2:15, 16, 18; 3:24, 36,
    49, 55, 61, 86, 116
  bull 3:61, 68
  calf 3:1, 24, 49, 86, 116
crab 1:12
  hermit 1:20

deer, roe 3:110
dog 2:97, 101
donkey 1:42; 2:48

elephant 1:82; 2:60
elk, Irish 3:72
ewe *see under* sheep

FISH:
  blenny 1:16
  brooktrout 1:55
  carp 2:87
  conger eel 1:4
  dab 1:53
  eel 3:92
  flounder 1:17
  loach 3:5, 21
  mackerel 3:8
  minnow 3:29
  pike 1:44; 3:11, 13, 53; 4:28
  salmon 3:73; 4:18, 41, 61, 64
  sea-trout 3:57; 4:55
  stickleback 1:34
  trout 3:21, 40; 4:41
foal *see under* horse

fox 1:38; 2:28, 40, 81, 103; 4:54
  Arctic 1:60
  vixen 2:80
frog *see* bullfrog

gander *see under* goose
goat 1:43; 2:71, 72, 74; 3:115
goose 2:29, 75, 78
  gander 2:40

hare 2:28, 89, 90, 91, 93, 95
  snow-shoe 1:56
hedgehog 2:88
hermit crab *see under* crab
horse 1:42; 2:20; 3:101; 4:32
  foal 2:11; 3:75
  pony 4:35
hyena 1:82

INSECTS:
  ant 1:58
  bee, honey 1:75; 2:51
  beetle 2:30
  blue-fly 3:89
  butterfly
    Red Admiral 1:31
    tortoiseshell 3:96
  caddis 3:48
  cranefly 3:84
  damselfly 3:70
  dragonfly 1:29
  flea 2:88
  fly 2:61, 63; 3:89
  gnat 4:7
  grasshopper 1:79
  honey bee 1:75; 2:51
  mayfly 3:94
  mosquito 3:14
  sandflea 1:6
  spider *see* spider

Irish elk *see* elk

jaguar 4:30, 56
jellyfish 1:13

kitten *see under* cat

lamb *see under* sheep
limpet 1:2
lion, mountain 3:95
lobster 1:5
lobworm *see under* worm

mermaid 1:1
mink 4:34
mole 1:41
moose 1:66
mountain lion 3:95
mouse 1:28; 2:58, 59
musk ox 1:70
mussel 1:21

octopus 1:15
otter 1:27; 4:52
ox, musk 1:70

pig 1:39; 2:41; 4:26
puma 1:68

rabbit 2:30
ragworm *see under* worm
ram *see under* sheep
rat 2:24, 29; 4:23

rhino, black 4:50

sea anemone 1:11
seal 1:22
sheep 1:32, 2:32, 33, 36; 3:15
  ewe 2:30; 3:45, 80
  lamb 2:31, 35, 36; 3:15,
    45, 80, 103
  ram 1:32, 2:30
shrew 1:49
shrimp 1:18
snail 1:26, 30
snow-shoe hare *see under* hare
spider 1:81; 3:30, 89
squirrel 1:46
starfish 1:10

tiger 3:109; 4:47
  tigress 3:9
toad 1:35

vixen *see under* fox
vole 2:29

weasel 2:56, 64, 84; 3:60
whale 1:3; 4:58
whelk 1:8
wolf 1:ix, 54, 64; 4:2, 39
wolverine 1:54
worm 1:25, 41; 2:83
  lobworm 2:111
  ragworm 1:14